REPENTANCE IS A GIFT

WRITTEN BY KATHLEEN GWILLIAM

ILLUSTRATED BY VICTORIA STARSKAIA

CFI • AN IMPRINT OF CEDAR FORT, INC. • SPRINGVILLE UTAH

Repent ye! Repent ye!
Has been each prophet's call.
Their teaching's been the same
Since the time of Adam's fall.

But what is repentance?
What does it really mean?
And how can it help you
Be happy, pure, and clean?

Repentance means to change
Your heart, mind, and behavior
To help you think like God
And act more like the Savior.

Repenting breaks bad habits
And helps your vices fall,
Like knocking down old buildings
With a wrecking ball.

When bad habits are removed
There's so much you can do.
You'll see that you are building
A wiser, stronger you.

Choosing to repent
Will heal the pain of sin.
The Savior looks inside
To mend you from within.

A doctor heals your arm
With an x-ray and a cast.
Christ will heal your heart
To leave sins in the past.

Like starting your game over
When things have gone astray.
Repenting helps you reset
To do things the right way.

You'll remember your mistakes
So your errors won't repeat.
But God will not recall them
When repentance is complete.

Sin will stain your spirit
Like grape juice on your clothes.
If the stain has not been treated,
The grape juice always shows.

Just like a stain remover
Christ's Atonement cleanses you.
You must turn to the Savior
To be as clean as new.

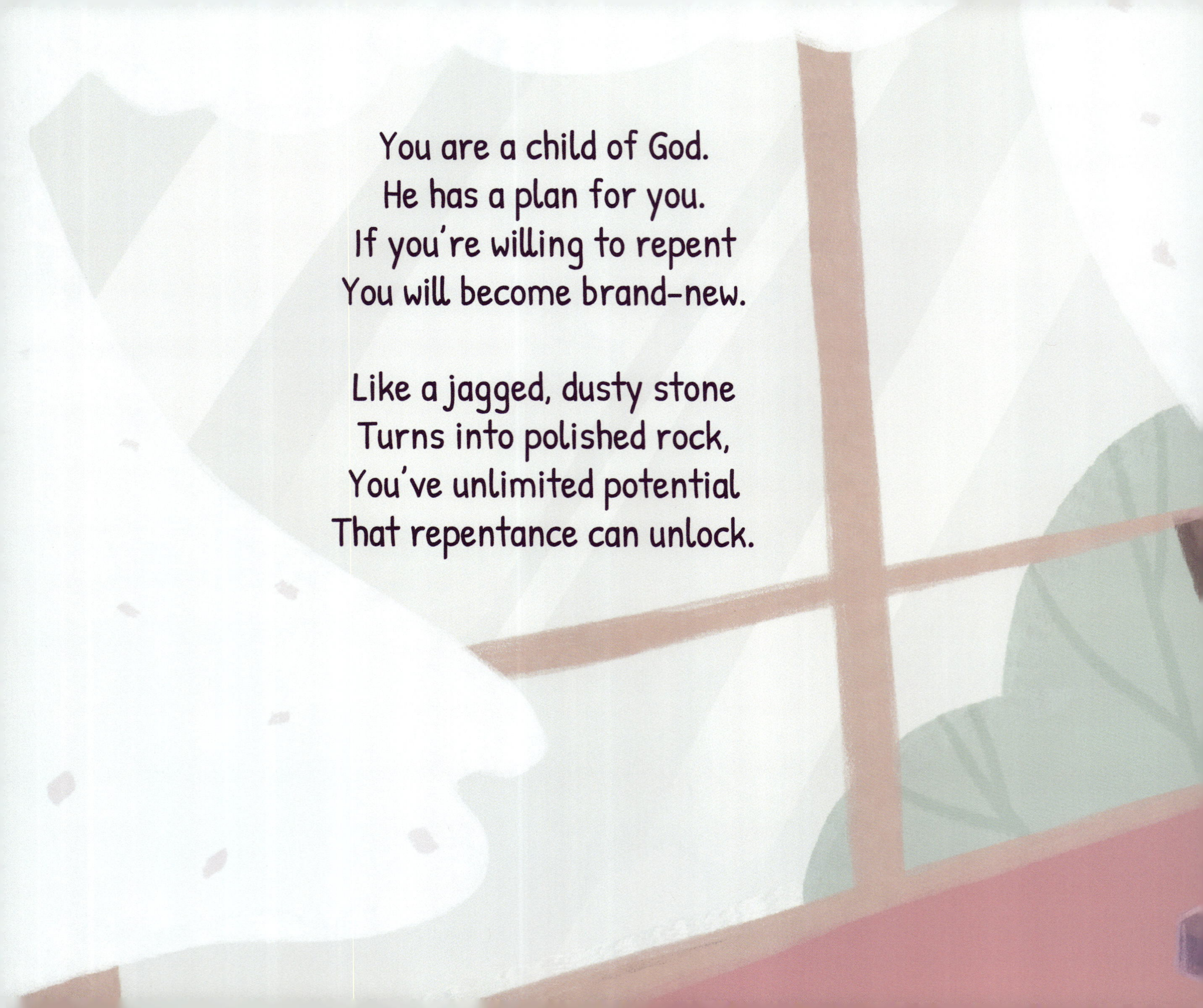

You are a child of God.
He has a plan for you.
If you're willing to repent
You will become brand-new.

Like a jagged, dusty stone
Turns into polished rock,
You've unlimited potential
That repentance can unlock.

Repentance brings you hope
As the Savior sends His light,
Like the sun piercing a storm
With rays so warm and bright.

That light is filled with love,
Forgiveness, joy, and peace.
It's all because of Him
That your guilt can be released.

We all need to repent
From mistakes that we have made.
Repentance starts with faith
That the price for sin's been paid.

Feel sorry and confess
And work to right the wrong.
Then learn from your mistakes.
Let faith and hope grow strong.

When repentance is complete,
Joy fills you from above
As the Holy Ghost delivers
Forgiveness and God's love.

Like the sweet taste of hot cocoa
That warms you from within,
The joy from true repentance
Helps real happiness begin.

Your journey back to God
Takes a slow and steady pace,
Filled with faith, hope, and repentance,
And plenty of God's grace.

When you reach your heavenly home
God's arms will open wide,
And the person you've become
You will not want to hide.

Repentance is a gift.
Its value can't be measured.
The chance to change and grow
Is a gift that must be treasured.

So utilize Christ's gift,
And each day you'll be forgiven.
You'll become what God intends
Through His gift that you've been given.

BREAK BAD HABITS: 2 Nephi 1:23

Shake off the chains with which ye are bound, and come forth out of obscurity, and arise from the dust.

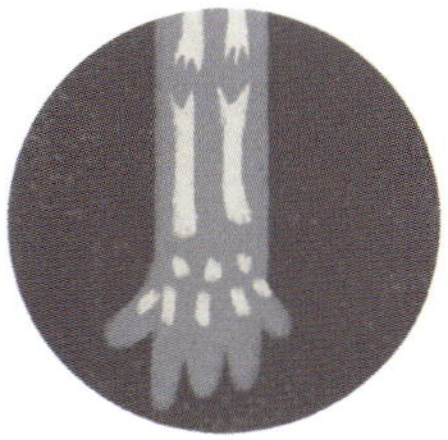

HEAL THE PAIN OF SIN: 3 Nephi 9:13–14

13 O all ye that are spared because ye were more righteous than they, will ye not now return unto me, and repent of
your sins, and be converted, that I may heal you?
14 Yea, verily I say unto you, if ye will come unto me ye shall have eternal life. Behold, mine arm of mercy is extended
towards you, and whosoever will come, him will I receive; and blessed are those who come unto me.

RESET YOUR LIFE: DOCTRINE AND COVENANTS 58:42

42 Behold, he who has repented of his sins, the same is forgiven, and I, the Lord, remember them no more.

CLEANED: ISAIAH 1:18

18 Come now, and let us reason together, saith the Lord: though your sins be as scarlet, they shall be as white as snow; though they be red like crimson, they shall be as wool.

TRANSFORMED: MORONI 10:32

32 Yea, come unto Christ, and be perfected in him, and deny yourselves of all ungodliness; and if ye shall deny yourselves of all ungodliness, and love God with all your might, mind and strength, then is his grace sufficient for you, that by his grace ye may be perfect in Christ; and if by the grace of God ye are perfect in Christ, ye can in nowise deny the power of God.

LIGHT AND FORGIVENESS: Alma 38:8–9

8 And it came to pass that I was three days and three nights in the most bitter pain and anguish of soul; and never,
until I did cry out unto the Lord Jesus Christ for mercy, did I receive a remission of my sins. But behold, I did cry unto
him and I did find peace to my soul.
9 And now, my son, I have told you this that ye may learn wisdom, that ye may learn of me that there is no other way or
means whereby man can be saved, only in and through Christ. Behold, he is the life and the light of the world. Behold,
he is the word of truth and righteousness.

STEPS OF REPENTANCE: Mosiah 10:10

10 And again, believe that ye must repent of your sins and forsake them, and humble yourselves before God; and ask
in sincerity of heart that he would forgive you; and now, if you believe all these things see that ye do them.

JOY OF REPENTANCE: Alma 36:18–20

18 Now, as my mind caught hold upon this thought, I cried within my heart: O Jesus, thou Son of God, have mercy on
me, who am in the gall of bitterness, and am encircled about by the everlasting chains of death.
19 And now, behold, when I thought this, I could remember my pains no more; yea, I was harrowed up by the memory of
my sins no more.
20 And oh, what joy, and what marvelous light I did behold; yea, my soul was filled with joy as exceeding as was my pain!

PATH TO GOD: 2 Nephi 31:17

17 Wherefore, do the things which I have told you I have seen that your Lord and your Redeemer should do; for, for
this cause have they been shown unto me, that ye might know the gate by which ye should enter. For the gate by which
ye should enter is repentance and baptism by water; and then cometh a remission of your sins by fire and by the Holy
Ghost.

THE GIFT: John 3:16

God so loved the world, that he gave his only begotten Son, that whosoever believeth in him should not perish, but have everlasting life.

To Jim, for supporting me through all my change.

—Kathleen

ISBN 13: 978-1-4621-3985-9

Published by CFI, an imprint of Cedar Fort, Inc.
2373 W. 700 S., Springville, UT 84663
Distributed by Cedar Fort, Inc., www.cedarfort.com

Cover design & Typesetting by Shawnda T. Craig

Printed in the United States of America

10 9 8 7 6 5 4 3 2 1

Printed on acid-free paper